Look! This Is Love

LOOK! THIS IS LOVE

Poems of Rumi

Translated by Annemarie Schimmel

Illustrated by Ingrid Schaar

SHAMBHALA

Boston & London

1991

Shambhala Publications, Inc.
Horticulture Hall
300 Massachusetts Avenue
Boston, Massachusetts 02115

Shambhala Publications, Inc.
Random Century House
20 Vauxhall Bridge Road
London SW1V 2SA

9   8   7   6   5   4   3   2   1

First Edition
Printed in Korea on acid-free paper
Distributed in the United States by Random House, Inc., in
Canada by Random House of Canada, Ltd, and in the
United Kingdom by Random Century Group

ISBN 0-87773-541-7   LC 91-9750

Contents

Introduction

JALALUDDIN RUMI (1207–1273), respectfully called Maulana, "Our Master," was born in present-day Afghanistan and spent most of his life in Konya in Anatolia (known as Rum, hence his surname, Rumi). The young professor of theology was transformed into a mystical poet through his meeting with Shamsuddin ("The Sun of Religion") of Tabriz, who led him to the zenith of mystical experience. In his longing for this Sun, who disappeared, temporarily and then forever, after a short stay in Konya, Maulana Rumi became a poet who poured out thousands of ecstatic verses at the sound of music, and often while whirling in enraptured dance. Untiringly he called the beloved:

> Not alone I keep on singing
>   Shamsuddin and Shamsuddin,
> But the nightingale in gardens
>   sings, the partridge on the hills.
> Day of splendor: Shamsuddin, and
>   turning heaven: Shamsuddin,
> Mine of jewels: Shamsuddin, and
>   Shamsuddin is day and night.

Hence the importance of the symbol of the sun in his poetry: it is an allusion to the friend's name; the friend who is both beautiful and dangerous like the sun. All of Rumi's verse is inspired, as he admits:

I think of rhymes, but my beloved says:
"Don't think of anything but of my
     face!"

Shams remained the immortal source of his inspiration, although later Maulana turned to the goldsmith Salahuddin to find himself again after the burning love of the Sun; then he turned back to this world to compose, on the request of his favorite disciple, Husamuddin Chelebi, the *Mathnavi*, "The Spiritual Couplets." This work, praised in the Persianate world as "the Koran in the Persian tongue," is a compendium of mystical experience, traditions, and folklore in more than 25,000 verses with no apparent "logical" order. Here, at the beginning of the work, Rumi insists that one's experiences must be told in veiled form:

It's better that the friend remain in veils!
You listen to the content of the tales:
It's better that His mysteries be told
In other people's stories, tales of old!

Seventeen years later, shortly before his
death, Rumi expressed the mystery of love once
more in his description of the loving woman
Zulaykha, whose every thought was directed to
the One, manifested in the beautiful Yusuf:

And when she said: "The wax is melting
    softly!"
That was to say: My friend was kind to
    me!
And when she said: "Look, how the
    moon is rising!"
And when she said: "The willow is now
    green!"

And when she said: "The leaves are a-
    trembling!"
And when she said: "How lovely burns
    the rue . . ."
And when she said: "The birds sang for
    the roses."
And when she said: "Beat firmly all my
    rugs!"
And when she said: "The bread is all
    unsalted!"
And when she said: "The spheres are
    going wrong . . ."
She praised something—that meant, "His
    sweet embracing."
She blamed something—that meant:
    "He's far away."

And when she piled up names and names
    and names—see:
Her sole intention was but Yusuf's
    name. . . .

Rumi's poetry, be it lyrical or epico-didactic, reflects this experience in ever-new images, in similes taken from daily life or in high-soaring verse, expressing the lover's feelings—longing, despair, or hope—in throbbing rhythms, rhythms of a heart that finds peace in remembering the beloved's name, in prayer and surrender, in mystical death, as symbolized in the movements of the Whirling Dervishes, who, inspired by his poetry, point by their ritual to the mystery of dying and being revived in Divine Love.

ANNEMARIE SCHIMMEL

Look! This Is Love

LOOK! THIS IS LOVE—to fly toward the
  heavens,
To tear a hundred veils in ev'ry wink,
To tear a hundred veils at the beginning,
To travel in the end without a foot,
And to regard this world as something
  hidden
And not to see with one's own seeing eye!
I said: "O heart, may it for you be blessèd
To enter in the circle of the lovers,
To look from far beyond the range of
  eyesight,
To wander in the corners of the bosom!
O soul, from where has come to you this
  new breath?
O heart, from where has come this heavy
  throbbing?

O bird, speak now the language of the birds
Because I know to understand your secret!"
The soul replied: "Know, I was in God's
    workshop
While He still baked the 'house of clay and
    water.'
I fled from yonder workshop at a moment
Before the workshop was made and created.
I could resist no more. They dragged me
    hither
And they began to shape me like a ball!"

Through love all that is bitter will be
   sweet.
Through Love all that is copper will be
   gold.
Through Love all dregs will turn to purest
   wine.
Through Love all pain will turn to
   medicine.
Through Love the dead will all become
   alive.
Through Love the king will turn into a
   slave!

FROM MYSELF I am copper,
    through You, friend, I am gold.
From myself I'm a stone, but
    through You I am a gem!

ONCE a beloved asked her lover: "Friend,
You have seen many places in the world!
Now—which of all these cities was the best?"
He said: "The city where my sweetheart
 lives!"

O SUN, fill our house once more with light!
Make happy all your friends and blind your
    foes!
Rise from behind the hill, transform the
    stones
To rubies and the sour grapes to wine!
O Sun, make our vineyard fresh again,
And fill the steppes with houris and green
    cloaks!
Physician of the lovers, heaven's lamp!
Rescue the lovers! Help the suffering!
Show but your face—the world is filled
    with light!
But if you cover it, it's the darkest night!

I SEE only your beauty,
    when I open my eyes,
I drink only your wine, dear,
    when I open my lips.
To talk with the people,
    that seems sinful to me—
When I talk about you, dear
    —long, so long, is my tale!
I am lame when they drag me
    on all ways and all roads;
On the way to your dwelling,
    there I race full of joy!
And my light is much greater
    than moonlight and sun
When I turn once my face
    to the King full of grace!

I've CHOSEN YOU, of all the world, alone!
Can You allow then that I sit and grieve?
My heart is in Your fingers like a pen:
You cause my sadness and You cause my
    joy.
What could I choose but that what You
    have chosen?
What do I see but that what You are
    showing?
Now You make grow from me a thorn,
    now roses—
Now I smell roses, now I feel the thorn.
When You keep me like that, that's how I
    am, friend!
When You want me like this—again, this
    is it.

And in the vat where our hearts are
    colored—
How would I find what love is, and what
    hatred?
You were the First and You will be the
    Last, too—
Let better be my end than my beginning!
When You are hidden, I'm an unbeliever;
When You are manifest, I'm a believer.
And I own nothing but what you have
    granted—
Why do You search my pockets and my
    sleeves?

MY HEART is an oyster,
   the friend's phantom: the pearl.
For me is no room left—
   for He fills the house!

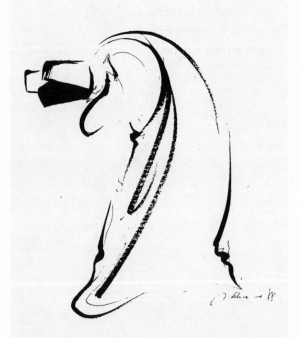

I'VE SEEN NO JOY without You in both
  worlds,
I've seen there wonders—nothing was like
  You.
I've put the soul's ear at the window
  "Heart"—
I've heard some words but never seen the
  lips!
You've lavished grace abundant on Your
  slave—
I've seen no reason but Your endless grace.
Cupbearer, dearer than my eyes, I have
Not seen one like You in Iran, Iraq!
Pour out such wine that I may leave
  myself—
I've only seen fatigue in my existence.

You're milk and You are sugar, sun and
    moon—
I've seen no family like You, my parent!
O endless Love, Divine manifestation—
I've seen no name that's worthy of You,
    Helper!
We are like iron scraps—Your love: the
    magnet.
You, without seeking, are the source of
    seeking!

WHEN YOU SEE THE SUN, remember
  the beloved's countenance!
When you see the cloud a-weeping,
  think of my, the servant's, tears!
When you see the fragile crescent
  that is melting just like me,
O remember, for your own sake,
  this weak soul that fades away!
Look up to the sky, regarding
  how the sphere is turning there
And remember how I'm turning,
  poor me, without hand and foot!
When you see how dark the world is
  from the night's black army now—
O remember those imprisoned
  here in separation's night!

When you see the star-bird Wega
    fiery, flying in the sky,
O remember those whose heart-bird
    sits with wings and feathers burnt!
When you see in the horizons
    Mars, the cruel, drinking blood—
O remember killing glances
    from those eyes that thirst for blood!

WHERE YOU PUT your foot on earth, my
   life,
Tulips, violets, and jasmine sprout.
If you take some clay and breathe on it,
It becomes a hawk, a dove, a crow!
If you wash your hand in earthen bowls
They become, thanks to your hand, pure
   gold.
If you say a prayer at a grave—
Look, a happy man lifts up his head!
If your garment strikes the claws of thorns,
They become a harp with sweetest sound.
Ev'ry idol that you smash, O friend,
Gets his soul and intellect from you.
If you shine on some ill-starred man—
Fortune's star relieves him from all pain!
Fifty verses would I like to sing,
But I close my mouth. You open yours!

بشنوا ین ز نی چون شکایت میکند

از جدا یی ها حکایت میکند

D. Khani 83

COME TO THE ROOF and look at the new
  moon!
Come in the garden, pluck an apple soon!
The apple grown in Anatolia—
Its fragrance reaches to the farthest East!
Come, harvest apples and draw forth your
  foot!
Spread furnishings from apples ruby-like!
I call him apple, or I call him wine,
And call him eglantine, narcissus fine.
It's all the same—what does he not possess?
O God! Preserve him well, O Lord—Amen!
Come now if you desire to hear a tale,
Come in and sit before me, candle-like.
I am afraid you may flee from the nook—
Come higher up and throw away your
  shoes!

Come, sit beside me! Tightly cling to me!
Give up your coquetry, your pride, your
    airs!
Come closer, O you mine of mercy, come!
So that your golden face turns colorful!
Do you permit? Although I do not speak
With blandishments and with false
    promises:
You are too pure for that, but lovers have
The tendency to speak confused words!

O SKY, don't revolve without me!
  O moon, do not shine without me!
O earth, do not go without me!
  O Time, do not go without me!
This world is enchanted by you,
  that world is enchanted by you—
Don't stay without me in this world!
  Don't go to that world without me!
Your face, yonder radiant moon
  makes lucid and lights our night—
I'm only the night, you're the moon. . . .
  Don't go to the spheres without me!
The rose, she is kind to the thorn
  and she protects him from fire—
Look, you are the rose, I'm the thorn!
  Don't go to your home without me!

I ASKED: "Dear Intellect, where are you?"
    And Intellect replied:
"Since I've turned into wine, why should I
    become a sour grape?"

LATE DID YOU COME—don't go away so
  soon!
Your going means: my soul departs from
  me!
Arriving late and soon departing, friend,
That is the custom of the rose in spring.
You asked: "How are you?" I am like a fish
That fell amidst the burning desert sand!
How would a city be, my prince, without
The justice and the order of the king?
I am not without you, but I desire
To be with you in perfect secrecy.
At night, the radiance of the sun is there,
Especially in hot nights in July,
The bats are happy merely with its heat
Because they fear the birds in daylight
  bright;

But birds—they want the light as well as
    heat
Because they are accustomed to the sun.
I talk of two distinguished kinds of birds—
Now, poet, look—to which do you belong?

Dɪᴅ I not say to you, friend:
  "Don't go, for I am your Friend?
I am the Water of Life
  in the mirage of decay!
And if in anger you go
  thousands of miles, far from me:
Finally you will return—
  I am your goal and your end!"
Did I not say to you, friend:
  "I am the sea, you're a fish.
Do not go to the dry land—
  I am the Attributes' sea!"
Did I not say to you, friend:
  "Don't fly like birds to the snare!
Come, I am strength for your flight,
  and I am strength for your wings!"

Did I not say to you, friend:
    "They'll block your road, make you cold!
But I am fire and heat,
    warmth of your heart and your love!"
Did I not say to you, friend:
    "Bad qualities, that's your share!
But you can lose them! I am
    the fountain of qualities pure."
Did I not say to you, friend:
    "Don't grieve: 'From which side my work
Will be arranged?' For I am
    He who creates, without sides!"

Look, I tried ev'rything, but nothing
    was lovelier than you,
And when I dived into the ocean,
    there was no pearl like you!
I open'd a thousand vats and barrels
    and tasted all of them,
But never was intoxicated
    by any wine but you.
How strange! There smile jasmine and roses
    with fragrance in my heart,
But never came close to my bosom
    the jasmine-breasted friend.
The pigeon "Heart" flies from my body
    up to your roof, my Soul,
And I complain like nightingales . . . for
    my pigeon stays with you!

IF YOU'RE A LOVER, leave all grief and
   sorrow!
Look at the wedding! Leave the mourning
   choir!
You be an ocean and throw out the boat!
You be a world and throw away the world!
Repent like Adam, regain Paradise
And leave behind you Adam's pit and jail!
Rise to the heaven as did Jesus once,
Leave back your donkey just as Jesus did!
And if you, Yusuf's lovers, cut your hands,
Then seize him, and thus find the healing
   balm!

Last night, I went before Him, full of
  heat.
He did not ask me, but sat calm and still.
I looked at Him; that meant: "Oh please,
  do ask:
'How have you been without my moonlike
  face?'"
My Friend, however, cast His eyes to earth:
"Be you like dust, so selfless and so low!"
I kissed the ground and fell upon my face;
That meant: I am bewildered like the dust!

UNDER THE SHADE of your tresses,
   how softly slept my heart,
Intoxicated and lovely,
   so peaceful and so free. . . .

IF WE SHOULD FILL the earth and sky with
   peace
And spread pure silver out before your
   dogs,
If for your king-bird that comes ev'ry morn
We'd lay a snare from souls and hearts and
   eyes,
And if we'd send a thousand hearts to you
That carry bloodstained letters in their
   hands,
And if we, for your sake, dwell in your fire
Like gold and silver to be purified—
Yet, by the Essence Pure! after all this
We look then ev'rywhere to find someone . . .
The end of this affair will come to this:
We call ourselves confused and stupefied,
And when the wine of the confused appears
We make a thousand cups from our heart,

And if the pure friend takes us to his
  breast,
Then we would tame that restive horse, the
  sky!

How do you know what birds we are?
What secretly we always sing?
Could anyone lay hands on us?
Now we are ruins, treasures now!
The sphere is turning for our sake—
That's why we also turn like spheres.
How could we stay here in this house?
For in this house we are all guests.
I look like beggars of the street—
Look inside: I'm a mighty king.
Tomorrow I am Egypt's king—
Why worry of my jail today?

دَرِ نيا بَذُ خَالِ يُحَتَّهِ هِيُج خَالِ

پَس مِحَن كُونَه بايِكُو السَّلام

I DIED a hundred times and I learned this:
Your fragrance came, and I was made alive.
I gave my life a hundred times, and fell—
I heard your call, and I was born again.
I placed a net to catch the falcon Love
Deep in my heart—he seized my heart, and
    went. . . .

WE ARE YOUR GUESTS, beloved Friend,
tonight.
What night? For we are Yours by day and
night!
For where we stay and where we go—we
are
Still present at Your table, near Your cup.
We are the pictures of Your artful hand,
We have been nourished by Your kindly
bread.
We are the baby pigeons of Your cote,
We circumambulate Your portico.
We set the gold ball in the sky a-dance.
Why not? We are the mallet in Your hand!
Let's be a mallet now, and now a ball,
As long as we stay in your polo ground!
Turn us into a serpent, or a rod—
Like Moses' miracle—we are Your proof!

Do open now our mouth and bind it too—
Yours is the binding, for we are Your bag!

It's the day of great joy,
    let us all become friends!
Let us join our hands,
    let us go to the Friend!
We are one and not two,
    of one color and hue,
Let us dance, let us go
    to the market a-dance!
For the beautiful friends
    are beginning to dance,
And we close our shop
    and are idle and free!
It's the day that the souls
    don the robe of His grace—
To the mysteries' side
    do we go as God's guests!

All the idols have pitched
    in the garden their tents,
And to see them, we go
    to the rose garden now!

I saw my friend; he wandered round the
  house;
He had a rebeck, and he played a tune.
He played a sweet tune with a touch of fire,
Intoxicated from the nightly wine.
He called the Saqi in the tune Iraqi—
That was but an excuse—he wanted wine.
The Saqi, moon-faced, in his hand a pitcher,
Came from the corner right toward the
  center.
He filled the first cup with the sparkling
  wine—
Have you seen fiery tongues that sprang
  from water?
He placed it on his hand for yonder lovers
And then he bowed and kissed the blessed
  threshold.

My friend took it from him and quaffed
    the wine,
And o'er his face the flashing flames were
    running,
And he beheld his radiant own beauty
And said a-smiling to the Evil Eye:
"There was no one, there will not be
    another
Like me in this age and in our time!"

Oh COME, oh come! You are the soul
   of the soul of the soul of whirling!
Oh come! You are the cypress tall
   in the blooming garden of whirling!
Oh come! For there has never been
   and will never be one like you!
Oh come! Such one have never seen
   the longing eyes of whirling!
Oh come! The fountain of the sun
   is hidden under your shadow!
You own a thousand Venus stars
   in the circling heavens of whirling!
The whirling sings your praise and thanks
   with a hundred eloquent tongues:
I'll try to say just one, two points
   translating the language of whirling.

For when you enter in the dance
    you then leave both these worlds.
For outside these two worlds there lies
    the universe, endless, of whirling.
The roof is high, the lofty roof
    which is on the seventh sphere,
But far beyond this roof has reached
    the ladder, the ladder of whirling!
Whatever there appears but He,
    you tread on that in dancing:
The whirling, see, belongs to you
    and you belong to the whirling.
What can I do when Love appears
    and puts its claw round my neck?
I grasp it, take it to my breast
    and drag it into the whirling!

And when the bosom of the motes
    is filled with the glow of the sun,
They enter all the dance, the dance
    and do not complain in the whirling!

Your countenance, O friend, is
   springtime smiling!
How lovely and how sweet, belovèd smiling!
I see you in eternal gardens, darling,
On branches as a pomegranate smiling.
Don't go away from me a single moment,
My sweetheart, you with lovely cheeks, and
   smiling!
The city "World" is ruined without you,
It is destroyed, O emperor all-smiling!
A hundred roses are in love with you
And wait near greenery and fountains
   smiling.
Your phantom in the forest of my heart:
A lion strong that seizes game a-smiling!
You always come from different directions
Just like the restless fortune ever smiling!

The qualities of Shams are like an ocean
That is replete with royal pearls, all smiling!

BLESSED TIME! when we are sitting,
    I and thou,
With two forms and only one soul,
    I and thou.
Fragrance, song of birds, they quicken
    ev'rything
When we come into the garden,
    I and thou.
All the stars of heaven hurry
    to see us,
And we show them our own moon,
    I and thou—
I and thou without words, without
    I and thou—
In delight we are united,
    I and thou.

Sugar chew the heaven's parrots
in that place
Where we're sitting, laughing sweetly,
I and thou.
Strange that I and thou together
in this nook
Are apart a thousand miles, see—
I and thou.
One form in this dust, the other
in that land,
Sweet eternal Paradise there . . .
I and thou.

THE MAN OF GOD is drunken without wine,
The man of God is full without roast meat.
The man of God is all confused, distraught,
The man of God needs neither food nor
    sleep.
The man of God: a king in dervish's frock,
The man of God: a treasure in the dust.
The man of God is not of air nor earth,
The man of God: of water not, nor fire.
The man of God, he is a boundless sea,
The man of God rains pearls without a
    cloud.
The man of God has hundred moons and
    skies,
The man of God has hundred radiant suns.
The man of God knows through the Truth
    Divine,
The man of God is learned without books.

The man of God: no heresy, nor faith,
The man of God knows not of wrong or
    right.
The man of God rode from Not-Being,
    look!
The man of God comes here in glorious
    state.
The man of God is hidden, Shamsuddin!
The man of God: You seek and find him,
    heart!

SAID SOMEONE: "Look, Master Sana'i is
  dead!"
Ah, such a man's death is no small affair!
He was no straw that is gone with the
  wind,
He was no water that froze in the cold,
He was no comb that broke in the hair,
He was no grain that was crushed by the
  earth.
He was a golden treasure in the dust
As he considered both the worlds a grain.
He cast the dust form back into the dust,
He carried heavenward both soul and mind.
The dregs were mixed here with the purest
  wine;
The wine then rose; the dregs were settling
  down.

The second soul, which people do not
  know—
By God! he gave it to the Friend, to God!
They all meet during travel, O my friend—
From Marw and Rayy, and Kurds, and
  Byzantine,
But ev'ryone returns to his own home—
Why should fine silk become a friend of
  wool?
Be quiet, quiet! For the King of Speech
Erased your name now from the book of
  speech!

THERE ROSE a moon on the sky
   in radiant morning time
And it came down from the sky
   and started gazing at me:
And like a falcon that hunts
   and snatches the little bird,
It seized me and grasped me and then
   it ran with me over the sky.
I looked at myself, and lo!
   I did no more see myself—
My body became in this moon
   by grace as subtle as souls.
I traveled thus in the soul;
   I saw nothing else but the moon:
Unveiled were the mysteries of
   primordial theophany.

And all the nine spheres of the sky
   had merged in this very moon—
The boat of existence was
   completely submerged in that sea.
The ocean billowed, and lo!
   Eternal Wisdom appeared
And cast a voice and cried out . . .
   That was how it was and became.
The ocean was all filled with foam,
   and every fleck of this foam
Produced a figure like this
   and was a body like that,
And every body-shaped fleck
   that heard a sign from that sea,
It melted and then returned
   into the ocean of souls.

تن ز جان و جان ز تن مستور نیست
لیک کس را دید جان دستور نیست

مثنوی
۱۹۹۰

But without the glorious strength
   of Shamsuddin, pride of Tabriz,
You could not behold yonder moon,
   you could never merge with the sea.

How should the soul not take wings
   when from the Glory of God
It hears a sweet, kindly call:
   "Why are you here, soul? Arise!"
How should a fish not leap fast
   into the sea from dry land
When from the ocean so cool
   the sound of the waves reached its ear?
How should the falcon not fly
   back to his king from the hunt
When from the falconer's drum
   it hears the call: "Oh, come back!"?
Why should not every Sufi
   begin to dance atom-like
Around the Sun of duration
   that saves from impermanence?

What graciousness and what beauty!
    What life-bestowing! What grace!
If anyone does without that, woe—
    what error, what suffering!
Oh fly, oh fly, O my soul-bird,
    fly to your primordial home!
You have escaped from the cage now—
    your wings are spread in the air.
Oh travel from brackish water
    now to the fountain of life!
Return from the place of the sandals
    now to the high seat of souls!
Go on! Go on! we are going,
    and we are coming, O soul,
From this world of separation
    to union, a world beyond worlds!

How long shall we here in the dust-world
   like children fill our skirts
With earth and with stones without value,
   with broken shards without worth?
Let's take our hand from the dust grove,
   let's fly to the heavens high,
Let's fly from our childish behavior
   and join the banquet of men!
Call out, O soul, to proclaim now
   that you are ruler and king!
You have the grace of the answer,
   you know the question as well!

OH, if a tree could wander
  and move with foot and wings!
It would not suffer the axe blows
  and not the pain of saws!
For would the sun not wander
  away in every night—
How could at ev'ry morning
  the world be lighted up?
And if the ocean's water
  would not rise to the sky,
How would the plants be quickened
  by streams and gentle rain?
The drop that left its homeland,
  the sea, and then returned—
It found an oyster waiting
  and grew into a pearl.

Did Yusuf not leave his father,
    in grief and tears and despair?
Did he not, by such a journey,
    gain kingdom and fortune wide?
Did not the Prophet travel
    to far Medina, friend?
And there he found a new kingdom
    and ruled a hundred lands.
You lack a foot to travel?
    Then journey into yourself!
And like a mine of rubies
    receive the sunbeams' print!
Out of yourself—such a journey
    will lead you to your self,
It leads to transformation
    of dust into pure gold!

Leave bitterness and all acid,
  go forth to sweetness now!
For even brine produces
  a thousand kinds of fruits.
It is the Sun of Tabriz
  that does such wondrous work,
For ev'ry tree gains beauty
  when touched by the sun.

HE SAID: "Who's knocking at my door?"
  Said I: "Your humble servant!"
Said He: "What business have you got?"
  Said I: "I came to greet You!"
Said He: "How long are you to push?"
  Said I: "Until You'll call me!"
Said He: "How long are you to boil?"
  Said I: "Till resurrection!"
I claimed I was a lover true
  and I took many oaths
That for the sake of love I lost
  my kingdom and my wealth!
He said: "You make a claim—the judge
  needs witness for your cause!"
Said I: "My witness is my tears,
  my proof my yellow face!"

Said He: "The witness is corrupt,
   your eye is wet and ill!"
Said I: "No, by Your eminence:
   My eye is sinless clear!"
He said: "And what do you intend?"
   Said I: "Just faithful friendship!"
Said He: "What do you want from me?"
   Said I: "Your grace abundant!"
Said He: "Who traveled here with you?"
   Said I: "Your dream and phantom!"
Said He: "And what led you to me?"
   Said I: "Your goblet's fragrance!"
Said He: "What is most pleasant, say?"
   Said I: "The ruler's presence!"
Said He: "What did you see there, friend?"
   Said I: "A hundred wonders!"

Said He: "Why is it empty now?"
  Said I: "From fear of brigands!"
Said He: "The brigand, who is that?"
  Said I: "It is that blaming!"
Said He: "And where is safety then?"
  Said I: "In renunciation."
Said He: "Renunciation? That's . . . ?"
  Said I: "The path to safety!"
Said He: "And where is danger, then?"
  Said I: "In Your love's quarters!"
Said He: "And how do you fare there?"
  Said I: "Steadfast and happy."
I tested you and tested you,
  but it availed to nothing—
Who tests the one who was once tried,
  he will repent forever!

Be silent! If I'd utter here
    the secrets fine he told me,
You would go out all of yourself,
    no door nor roof could hold you!

OH SEIZE the hem of His favor,
　　for suddenly He will flee!
But do not draw Him like arrows,
　　for from the bow He will flee.
Look—all the shapes He assumes, and
　　what kind of tricks He plays!
In form He may well be present,
　　but from the soul He will flee.
You seek Him high in His heaven—
　　He shines like the moon in a lake,
But if you enter the water,
　　up to the sky He will flee.
You seek Him in Where-no-place is—
　　then He gives signs of His place:
But if you seek Him in places,
　　to Where-no-place He will flee.

As arrows fly from the bowstring
     and like the bird of your thought . . .
You know for sure: from the doubting
     the Absolute One will flee.
"I'll flee from this and from that, see—
     but not out of weariness:
I fear that My beauty, so lovely,
     from this and from that may well flee.
For like the wind I am flighty,
     I love the rose, like the breeze,
But out of fear of the autumn,
     you see, the rose too will flee!"
His name will flee when it sees you
     intent on pronouncing it
So that you cannot tell others:
     "Look here, such a person will flee!"

He'll flee from you if you try then
    to sketch His picture and form—
The picture flees from the tablet,
    the sign from the heart will flee!

DEEP-FROZEN stays the ice in shady places
Which did not see the radiance of my Sun.
But ev'ry ice that saw the sun-face smiling
Says, melting: "I'm the water that grants
    life."

O YOU WHOSE NAME is food for drunken
   souls,
And days with whom illuminate my mind!
My pale face turned the world into pure
   gold
Until I saw your shining silver limbs!
You said: "My heart is worried for your
   sake!"
I don't wish anything but what you wish!
I sit here, waiting, near the door until
Your message comes: "I'll take your soul
   away!"

IF DEATH'S A MAN, let him come close to me
That I can take him tightly to my breast!
I'll take from him a soul, pure, colorless—
He'll take from me a colored frock, that's
    all.

Now you've departed and gone to the
Unseen—

On what strange ways you've gone from our
world!

You shook your feathers and you broke the
cage;

You flew away, far, to the soul's own
world.

You were a hawk, encaged by Mrs.
World—

You heard the drum and flew to Where-no-
place.

You were a nightingale among the owls—

The garden's scent came; you went to the
rose.

You suffered headache from these bitter
dregs—

At last you went to the eternal tavern. . . .

The rose flees from the autumn—daring
   rose
That you went on in the autumnal wind!
You fell like rain on the terrestrial roof,
Run here and there, escaping through the
   spout.
Be silent—there is no more pain of
   speaking:
You are protected by a loving friend!

THE DAY I've died, my pall is moving on—
But do not think my heart is still on earth!
Don't weep and pity me: "Oh woe, how
    awful!"
You fall in devil's snare—woe, that is awful!
Don't cry "Woe, parted!" at my burial—
For me this is the time of joyful meeting!
Don't say "Farewell!" when I'm put in the
    grave—
A curtain is it for eternal bliss.
You saw "descending"—now look at the
    rising!
Is setting dangerous for sun and moon?
To you it looks like setting, but it's rising;
The coffin seems a jail, yet it means freedom.
Which seed fell in the earth that did not
    grow there?
Why do you doubt the fate of human seed?

What bucket came not filled from out the
  cistern?
Why should the Yusuf "Soul" then fear this
  well?
Close here your mouth and open it on that
  side
So that your hymns may sound in Where-
  no-place!

OH HAPPY DAY when in your presence,
    my ruler, I shall die!
When near the sugar-treasure melting
    like sugar I shall die!
Out of my dust will grow a thousand
    of centifolias
When in the shade of yonder cypress
    in gardens I shall die.
And when you pour into my goblet
    the bitter drink of death,
I'll kiss the goblet full of joy, dear,
    and drunken I shall die.
I may turn yellow like the autumn
    when people speak of death,
Thanks to your smiling lip: like springtime
    and smiling shall I die.

I have died many times, but your breath
    made me alive again,
Should I die thus a hundred more times
    I happily shall die!
A child that dies in mother's bosom,
    that's how I am, my friend,
For in the bosom of His Mercy
    and kindness, I shall die.
Say: Where would death be for the lovers?
    Impossible is that!
For in the fountain of the Water
    of Life—there I shall die!

LEARN FROM God's Messenger this alchemy:
Be satisfied with what He gives to you.
And when the envoy "Grief" comes to your
   house,
Then take him to your breast like an old
   friend!

WEAVE NOT, like spiders, nets from grief's
    saliva
In which the woof and warp are both
    decaying.
But give the grief to Him, Who granted it,
And do not talk about it anymore.
When you are silent, His speech is your
    speech,
When you don't weave, the weaver will be
    He.

AND IF HE CLOSES before you
the ways and passes all—
He'll show a hidden pathway
which nobody has known!

Notes

p. 8   The "friend" in Rumi's poetry usually refers to Shamsuddin, but as he appears as the locus of manifestation of the Divine Friend, one cannot always sharply distinguish between a love poem and a prayer poem.

p. 10   The story of Yusuf and Zulaykha is found in the Koran, Sura 12; it is also well known in the story of Joseph as told in Genesis 37–40. The beautiful young man was cast into a well by his jealous brothers, rescued, and sold as a slave in Egypt, where Potiphar's wife—called Zulaykha in the Islamic tradition—fell in love with him and tried to seduce him. When this love made her the object of scorn and blame, Zulaykha invited her friends to her house and served them oranges. While the ladies were peeling the oranges with knives, Yusuf appeared, and, gazing at his beauty, they cut off their hands instead: One does not feel pain when beholding the beauty of the friend. (This episode is referred to in the poem on page 43.) Yusuf was imprisoned but eventually rose to the office of the highest administrator in Egypt.

p. 21   Houris are paradisiacal virgins, clothed—like all spiritual beings—in green garments. When spring comes and the earth is fresh and green, it looks as if messengers from Paradise have arrived.

p. 30   The Wega is called in Arabic "the descending eagle," hence the comparison to the bird.

p. 31   In lines 3–4, the beloved is implicitly compared to Jesus, who quickened the dead and made birds of clay come to life with his breath. This comparison is commonplace in Persian poetry.

p. 57   Saqi is the "cupbearer" who offers the wine of love to the lovers. Iraqi is a musical mode.

p. 66   Parrots are said to be "sugar-chewing" because they are able to speak with sweet words. Their green color classifies them as birds associated with Paradise.

p. 70   Sana'i (died in 1131 in Ghazna, present-day

Afghanistan) was the first Persian mystical poet to use the form of the *mathnavi*, "rhyming couplets," for a didactic work. His poetry influenced Rumi deeply.

p. 71   Marw is a city in northeastern Iran; Rayy is now part of the city of Tehran. The phrase "Marw and Rayy" means two places that are very far apart.

p. 77   "The place of the sandals" is the place in the back where one leaves one's shoes when entering a house or mosque; there only lowly people would sit.

SHAMBHALA CENTAUR EDITIONS are named for a classical modern typeface designed by the eminent American typographer Bruce Rogers. Modeled on a fifteenth-century Roman type, Centaur was originally an exclusive titling font for the Metropolitan Museum of Art, New York. The first book in which it appeared was Maurice de Guérin's *The Centaur*, printed in 1915.

Until recently, Centaur type was available only for handset books printed on letterpress. Its elegance and clarity make it the typeface of choice for Shambhala Centaur Editions, which include outstanding classics of the world's literary and spiritual traditions.